# Xposed: Unmasking the Man of the Stars

## Celestial Secrets Revealed

Tom Levy

First edition: November 2023

ISBN: 978-2-89864-025-4

Published by: 01 Web Canada

# Preface

In a universe where reality often surpasses fiction, the life and achievements of Elon Musk often seem to border on the unimaginable. From a humble childhood in South Africa to his role as a pioneer of the new frontiers of technology and space, Musk's trajectory has continuously captivated the entire world.

This book is a humorous, sometimes profound, exploration of the life of this exceptional man. As you flip through these pages, you will not only discover Musk's accomplishments but also a series of playful and comedic theories attempting to explain his genius. Is he truly of our world, or could he be the ambassador of a distant civilization, sent to guide humanity?

From the early days of SpaceX to the promise of Neuralink, through the intrigues of The Boring Company and the possible extraterrestrial imprint behind every tweet, each chapter is designed to make you smile, reflect, and marvel. Yet, beyond the humor, this book is also a celebration of audacious innovations, futuristic dreams, and Musk's vision.

In "Xposed : Unmasking the Man of the Stars", we affectionately and admiringly demystify the man behind the legend. As a reader, expect to be transported across the cosmos, through laughter and moments of sheer astonishment. Happy reading and enjoy the journey on this intergalactic adventure!

# Table des matières

# Chapter 1:
# Musk's Origin Story

It In the vast expanse of our boundless universe, amidst twinkling stars, majestic nebulae, and never-ending galaxies, a peculiar event was unfolding. The night sky, with its shimmering canvas, was gearing up for one of its grandest performances. Somewhere in the galactic lane between Alpha Centauri and the Milky Way, a silvery pod zoomed along, bending the rules of physics as we know them. Its target? A little blue-green marble known as Earth.

On the evening of its descent, nothing was business as usual. Above the South African town of Pretoria, known in interstellar circles as "Earth's Premier Pit-Stop," clouds were crafting some quirky patterns. Hexagons, spirals, and yes, even barcodes danced across the night, as if the heavens were processing a celestial checkout.

To the untrained human eye, this might've seemed like just another weather anomaly. But in truth, it marked SpaceX's maiden terrestrial drop-off. And the package? Not some high-tech alien gizmo, but a radiant tiny tot, clutching a cosmic handbook titled "How to Human: The Ultimate Guide for Starry Entities."

The capsule, soaring over vast terrains, pinpointed Pretoria for its landing and gently touched down, emitting a soft 'ping' upon impact. The townsfolk gathered round, half-expecting a shout of "It's Amazon!" But instead, they found a baby - Elon, making his entrance with all the subtlety of a spaceship crash-landing in the heart of town.

The peculiar appearance of this silvery pod didn't slip under the radar. In fact, no fewer than 19 folks reported the spectacle to local law enforcement, recounting in astonishment about a "heavenly vehicle" descending onto Pretoria's plains. These accounts, as diverse as they were detailed, spoke of shimmering lights, a muffled thud, and the enigmatic infant found nestled within the capsule.

"Galaxy24 TV" broadcast a special segment on the matter, dubbed "Pretoria Puzzle: The Starry Visitor." Reporters were on the scene, grilling witnesses, including a local farmer who claimed to have spotted "barcodes in the sky" and a schoolteacher swearing the tiny tot had what seemed like a cosmic navigation manual in his grasp.

The "Pretoria Daily Times," one of the prominent local newspapers, dedicated a good chunk of its front page to this peculiar event, with catchy headlines like "Star Child" and "The Night Pretoria Met the Cosmos." The paper also rolled out an in-depth probe, aiming to unearth the truth behind this mysterious touchdown.

However, despite the evident public intrigue and numerous detailed accounts, the local authorities seemed keen on hushing things up. Black trucks, devoid of any markings, began patrolling the streets of Pretoria. Key witnesses were questioned behind closed doors, and some even claimed they were persuaded not to discuss what they had witnessed that fateful night. The landing site itself was swiftly fenced off and guarded, while local officials continued to deny any out-of-the-ordinary occurrence.

But, try as they might, the cat was out of the bag. The folks of Pretoria knew they had witnessed something extraordinary, unexplained—a night when the stars themselves seemed to graze the Earth.

The Musks, local residents already known for their quirks (after all, they had a pet meerkat named Zog), lived closest to the landing spot. And while they were expecting a delivery—a brand-new solar toaster—what they got was a whole lot more electrifying. A baby. Elon. The universe's gift to Earth. A child destined to reshape humanity's view of the cosmos.

From a young age, Elon stood out from the toddler crowd. While most kids dreamt of candy and toys, he was engrossed in musings about rocket propulsion and energy grids. At five, instead of playing house, he tried to build a sustainable treehouse, fitted with solar panels and a wind turbine. His attempts at constructing a windmill were a tad clumsy; once, he used an umbrella as a turbine, and every time it rained, his "power plant" doubled as an impromptu bird shelter, sending the neighborhood kids into fits of laughter. But Elon, far from being disheartened, saw it as an opportunity to study bird habits up close.

His school days were nothing short of out-of-this-world. During "show and tell", while his pals brought in turtles or showcased their stamp collections, Elon would roll in with a hyperloop prototype. One buddy, seeing the intricate designs, piped up, "Is that a fancy new hover-vacuum?"

The teacher, slightly taken aback, gave him an "A" with a cheeky note: "Very imaginative. Maybe too much so? And if you do manage that flying vacuum, my floors would be forever in your debt!"

Whispers began to swirl. Was Elon truly from our blue planet? Everything seemed to add up—his never-ending curiosity, unyielding drive to innovate, and that peculiar penchant for staring at the red dot in the night sky (Mars, for the uninitiated). Village gossip went wild: "Is he here to save us? Gearing up Earth for some cosmic masterplan? Or did he just pop by for the free Wi-Fi?"

The conjecture didn't stop there. Some village elders, gathered around campfires under starry nights, spoke of an ancient prophecy. They murmured he hailed from Mars, but the wiser ones wagered that this "star-child" came from a planet beyond the asteroid belt, maybe even the exoplanet "Muskania" in the Zepter11 galaxy—a place rumored to have LED fairy lights twinkle naturally at night, and where rivers flowed with... pumpkin-spiced almond milk. These old-timers spun tales of a land where gravity was so intense, everyone naturally had to "think outside the box" lest they get squashed, all while dodging the occasional caramel latte downpours.

Kids, by flashlight, dreamt up his home as a realm of half-robot, half-human beings, where electric cars ruled the roads, and the prime pastime was augmented reality space trivia. The braver souls reckoned that Elon's distant planet had already put their flag on other worlds, and Earth was just their latest sandbox.

But one wild guess really took the apple pie: Was Elon just an interstellar traveler hunting for the universe's best apple tart? After all, isn't that the ultimate quest for every enlightened being?

As these tales and musings swirled, Elon kept aiming for the stars. Rockets, electric cars, underground tunnels—it seemed there wasn't a field he didn't want to shake up. But at the heart of it all was the cosmic jest only he was in on. For while Earth debated his genius, his real mission was just revving up.

Maybe he was Earth's guardian, sent to launch humanity into a sparkling interstellar future. Or perhaps he was just here on a vacay, and all this innovation was just him doodling. The plot thickens. But as this story unfolds, remember this: The universe, in all its grandeur, has a peculiar punchline. And Elon? Maybe he's just the universe's wink and nudge.

# Chapter 2:
# Early Signs

**A Provincial Little Prodigy**

In the quaint town of Pretoria, where valleys bask in the sun and the occasional majestic creature roams, young Elon was growing up... or should I say, "acclimating." His earthly abode was humble, nestled between baobabs and jacarandas, just a stone's throw from chirping birds and the roar of the African savanna. Yet for Elon, these earthly tunes were always accompanied by a gentle hum – a frequency only he could pick up, a sweet reminder of his starry roots.

Right from the start, there were... oddities. While most kids played in humble sandboxes, Elon had the vast expanse of his imagination as his playground. He could spend hours, eyes glued to the azure sky, sketching geometric patterns on the ground that eerily resembled... advanced calculus equations. His fingers outlined futuristic cities and astonishingly advanced propulsion systems.

One day, young Elon, driven by insatiable curiosity, stumbled upon the family toaster. For the average Joe, it was a breakfast tool. For Elon? His first "encounter" with human tech. Within minutes, the toaster was in bits. Not broken, mind you, but disassembled with Swiss watchmaker precision. So, what does Elon do with a disassembled toaster on the kitchen table? Well, he did what he always does: revolutionize.

While for most of us, the pinnacle of toaster innovation would be achieving perfectly golden toast, Elon had other plans. With some tweaks here and additions there, our dear alien had transformed the humble toaster into a futuristic device capable not only of toasting bread, but also buttering and jamming it, while keeping it warm until you're ready to munch.

Plus, it now came with an AI feature. It could chat with you, update you with the day's news, or even suggest recipes based on your fridge contents. The "ToastoTalk," as he fondly named it, became the morning's main attraction.

One might think it would stop there, but nope. Rumors buzzed that this enhanced toaster was the prototype for a range of smart kitchen appliances Elon was thinking of rolling out. A blender teaching you salsa as it preps your smoothie? A kettle serenading you with Pavarotti as it boils your water? With Elon, anything's on the table.

The world was abuzz, waiting to see what everyday object this genius would transform next. But one thing was certain: thanks to Elon, no toaster would ever be looked at in the same way again. Who would have thought that a simple kitchen appliance could become a symbol of human ingenuity... or should I say, extraterrestrial?

**Human and Musk-querade**

But his enthusiasm didn't stop there. Radios, televisions, the early beginnings of computing; all underwent the same curious fate in the hands of this Pretoria genius. Every gadget became a puzzle, a challenge to understand and then enhance. A memorable episode involved the family's old TV. After one of Elon's "interventions," the device not only picked up local channels but also seemed to intercept signals from distant galaxies, broadcasting interstellar games where participants floated in zero gravity.

As Elon "aged" (or "simulated aging," as some local conspiracy theorists whispered), his relationship with technology became legendary. His school's computer lab? Transformed. Under his touch, those old computers, which crashed at the mere thought of running a game as basic as 'Pong', now simulated multi-planetary environments. And a strange new feature appeared: the "Mars Mode." No one really knew what it was for, but the red screen it displayed was oddly soothing.

During his teenage years, an event made a significant impression. On a school trip to a local observatory, Elon was particularly fascinated by a vast telescope pointed at the stars. Where his peers saw clusters of stars and distant galaxies, Elon saw... opportunities. Or rather, destinations. The guide, an elderly astronomer, exclaimed in puzzlement: "It's strange. Every time he looks through the lens, our equipment beeps as if detecting an unidentified object."

**First Steps into a Larger Universe**

But it wasn't just with technology that Elon seemed in sync. He always appeared to be gearing up for something momentous. Each of his "projects," whether transforming a bike into an energy generator or broadcasting announcements in multiple (and apparently extraterrestrial) languages over the school's sound system, seemed like a step. Preparatory training for an as-yet-unknown mission.

His peers often joked, half in admiration and bewilderment, that Elon was working on "alien missions." And young Musk, ever in the loop, would reply with a wink: "You have no idea."

Indeed, while most teens dreamt of dates and video games, Elon's nights were filled with visions of reinvented rockets and interplanetary voyages. These weren't mere daydreams; they were visions. Almost prophecies. Glimpses of a future he alone could perceive and perhaps alone could bring about.

Every gizmo he touched, every tech he altered, bore Elon's unmistakable stamp. Always enhanced, always optimized, and always... a touch extraterrestrial. These early signs, these singular interactions with the everyday, were but a teaser. A sketch of the interstellar symphony to come.

For in the heart of Pretoria, amid the crickets' song and the distant roar of lions, a prodigy from another world was emerging. A starry boy on a blue planet, gearing up for a destiny that would tie galaxies together. And as the sun set over the African plains, the cosmic dance was only beginning.

# Chapter 3:
# His Interstellar Ventures

## SpaceX: A Subtle Hint?

The new millennium was dawning on Earth, and with it, a new enterprise sprang from Musk's extraordinary mind. Enter SpaceX - or as some whispered in the shadow of the rockets, "Space eXtraterrestrial."

The public thought that SpaceX aimed to reduce space transportation costs and make Mars habitable for humans; a noble endeavor, certainly, but between the lines and beneath the metal of the Falcon rockets, was there a bigger secret? Was SpaceX Musk's audacious project to not only touch the stars but to... reconnect with his kin?

Each launch seemed less a technological feat than a cosmic message, a beacon. What if, in the vast expanses of the universe, these rockets signaled his celestial kin: "I am here. Look how far I've come. Are you watching?"

**The Falcon's Flight**

The Falcon rockets were prodigious. Reusable, majestic, their efficiency sent shivers down the spine. Their return to Earth, more a celestial dance than an engineering marvel. Rumors circulated: was the name "Falcon" a nod to a cosmic entity, the "Falcon Nebula"?

**Starlink: A Galactic Direct Line?**

Then came Starlink. Officially, a constellation of satellites aimed at providing high-speed internet access to every corner of the Earth. Promotional videos showcased remote villages, previously devoid of the magic of the web, joyfully diving into the digital world. But for a certain segment of the population, this explanation seemed... simplistic.

In reality, for the followers of "Musk-ism," the theory went much deeper. There were murmurs, hushed discussions in the dark corners of the Internet. Starlink, they said, was less a gateway to the universal World Wide Web and more a direct line to the cosmos. After all, with such satellite coverage, who could definitively say that Musk wasn't extending antennas towards his home planet, Muskania?

One evening, Tania DuBois, a famous podcaster and conspiracy theorist, proposed that each Starlink satellite had an encrypted channel. A channel that, instead of broadcasting memes and cat videos, served as a bridge to the Zepter11 galaxy. She cheekily suggested that every time we sent an "alien" emoji from our smartphones, we were actually sending a warm greeting to our extraterrestrial neighbors.

This theory became so popular that it spawned a new trend: "Hello Musk-anian" parties. Attendees would lie in their gardens, pointing their phones to the sky, flooding the atmosphere with coded messages in hopes of an interstellar reply. For most, it was just fun, but for a few, it was the hope of a sign, a wink from the neighboring galaxy.

**The Bigger Picture**

Every move Musk made, every company he launched, every satellite he orbited... Everything seemed to fit meticulously into a vast cosmic mosaic. The puzzle pieces were falling into place, slowly but surely revealing a grand tableau that only a mind as expansive and adventurous as his could conceive.

The more romantic theorists maintained that Musk was seeking to establish a bridge between his distant birth planet, Muskania, and Earth, hoping to create a symbiosis between the two worlds. Others believed he was preparing our world for a potential encounter with other civilizations, ensuring Earth wouldn't be left behind in the grand intergalactic scheme.

Whatever the truth, one thing was certain: Elon Musk was not just an entrepreneur. He was a visionary, a dreamer, and perhaps, just perhaps, the most famous alien Earth has ever known.

# Chapter 3: Tesla & The Electric Extraterrestrial

**Why Aliens Go Green (and Not Just Their Skin!)**

In the immense universe, where stars shimmer like glitzy disco balls at a space-themed party, one thing was universally agreed upon — party sustainably or not at all. This was a lesson many star-hopping societies learned the hard way. They realized, if you party too hard without thinking of tomorrow, the hangover can be, well, apocalyptic. And so, they decided: To party forever, you need to groove with nature.

Enter Musk. Was he Earth's DJ, spinning the discs of sustainable energy? Why else would he be so hooked on the electric beat? Tesla wasn't just another car on the block — it was the life of the party!

Now, why did Elon send a Tesla to space? A clever PR stunt or was there a deeper (or should we say, higher) motive?

**Interstellar Carpooling, Anyone?**

Whispers among the galaxy's most elite, well-groomed UFOlogists suggest that the Tesla in space was actually Musk's interstellar Uber invitation! Yep, believe it or not, even on Mars or in the Alpha Centauri star system, aliens who love green are all about carpooling. But here's the twist — their space-Ubers were always packed, and they desperately needed a snazzy, eco-friendly ride to their annual Black Hole Sustainability Conference.

Elon, ever the cosmic opportunist, saw a golden ticket. Sending his Tesla into space was his way of saying, "Hey, extraterrestrials! We Earthlings can be cool and green too!" And who knows? Maybe an alien, seeing that floating Tesla, waved and thought, "Why not? It's electric!" Then, plugging in his galactic playlist, and humming to David Bowie's tunes, off he went, zooming through the Milky Way.

So, next time you spot a glimmer in the night sky, just think — it might be that Tesla, with an alien jamming to "Space Oddity" at the wheel. All thanks to the vision of one man: Elon Musk. Or should we say... Elon the Alien? 🛸🚗.

## Auto-Pilot: More Than Just Cruise Control?

Underneath the star-studded quilt of the night sky, whispers from the universe seem to hint at age-old secrets. And amid these whispers, one question echoed louder: How did Tesla's Autopilot go from 0 to sci-fi, real quick?

When Elon showcased Autopilot, the world's jaw dropped. Cars that could navigate, dodge, read signs, and go with the flow? It seemed otherworldly. But could this tech marvel be, perhaps, not of this world?

Some spacethusiasts reckon the Autopilot tech might not be purely a Musk original but maybe a galactic hand-me-down. They suggest that UFOs, buzzing about for decades, have some nifty self-flying tech. So, did extraterrestrial Elon tap into ancient starry know-how for Autopilot?

The evidence, though starlight thin, is intriguing. How did Tesla's tech zoom ahead so fast? Why couldn't other car giants, despite their years in the fast lane, catch up? And why does Elon seem so sure, almost as if he's got an ace up his space-sleeve?

Perhaps the real magic behind Autopilot isn't in Tesla's labs but amongst the twinkling stars.

Imagine a future where Autopilot doesn't just help us dodge Earthly traffic but zips us from one galaxy to another. Maybe, just maybe, Tesla's grand plan isn't just about mastering Earth's highways but the cosmic freeway.

Gazing at the Milky Way, it's hard not to dream big. And as Elon might quip, "When you shoot for the stars, why not take the galaxy too?" With Tesla's Autopilot, the universe seems just an electric glide away.

**The Silent Song of Sustainability**

Behind the gentle purr of the electric engines, if you tuned in, there was a galactic anthem — a song of hope. As night blankets the world, Teslas, with their ambient glow, stood like electric knights, guarding the dawn of a new age. An age where Earth, with its star-man Musk at the helm, finds its groove in the cosmic dance.

# Chapter 4: Neuralink – Decoding Human Minds

## The 'Alien Technology' He Wants to Implant

In a world still grappling with the mysteries of its own biological wonders, Musk introduced Neuralink, a venture that promised to bridge the gap between the human brain and machines. As if electric cars and rockets weren't enough, Musk now wanted to tap directly into our very essence, our minds. But what was the story behind this audacious endeavor?

Across the vast cosmos, advanced civilizations had long since evolved past mere verbal communication. They communicated through thought, through pulses of understanding, transcending the barriers of language. The 'Neuralace,' as it was called in some star clusters, was an intricate weave of nano-threads that enveloped the brain, allowing beings to connect, communicate, and even control devices through mere thought.

When Musk spoke of the Neuralink chip and its potential, those with an interstellar inkling saw familiar echoes. Was this Neuralink a primitive version of the 'Neuralace'? Was Musk trying to usher in a new era of communication, taking a page out of the intergalactic playbook?

The Neuralink device, with its delicate threads promising to intertwine with the human brain, seemed too advanced, too outlandish for contemporary Earth technology. Its design, resembling a coin with delicate tendrils, was eerily similar to ancient artifacts discovered on distant planets. Artifacts that held the power to unlock minds, to share memories, to weave stories across millennia.

**User Testimonials (Secrets of Neuralink)**

In the darkest corners of the web, startling testimonials are beginning to emerge—tales from Neuralink users that defy all reason. Secured through covert means, these accounts seem to have captured the attention of the highest echelons of government. Multiple sources claim these individuals are under close watch by the NSA and other intelligence agencies, fueling theories that they might possess knowledge beyond human comprehension. Some even whisper that the figures trailing them aren't mere agents, but beings from beyond. Before you embark on this journey through their stories, be warned: once you dive into these testimonials, there's no turning back. And who knows who might start watching... you?

**Tim, 35, Accountant:**

"Ever since I got Neuralink, I've been doing my taxes in nanoseconds. But the weirdest part? Now, every time I see numbers, I hear a faint voice in my head chanting, 'One with the universe, one with the balance sheet.' Thanks, Elon?"

**Joe Rogan, 56 years old, Podcast Host:**

"I've always had an insatiable curiosity. With Neuralink, it's been taken to the next level. During my interviews, I can feel my guests' emotions before they even express them. And sometimes, during my podcast, I pick up on unknown frequencies, making me feel like I'm hosting a show for the entire galaxy. Sometimes, during my podcast, I pick up on frequencies that sound suspiciously like aliens discussing their favorite kettlebell workouts. And, you know what? I'm secretly hoping the next Neuralink update includes a 'DMT trip' setting. Just imagine, tripping without the trip to the Amazon!  It would be insane!"

**Eddie Bravo, 152 years old, PhD in conspiracy theory:**

"Ever since I got Neuralink, every time I close my eyes, I get these incredibly sharp images of Earth... but it's flat! And whenever I try to challenge this vision, a soft, extraterrestrial voice whispers to me: 'Trust your instincts, Eddie.' I knew I was right! But now, I'm starting to wonder if Elon is really on our side or if he's playing some cosmic game on another level..."

**Mr Beast, 29 years old, Philanthropic YouTuber:**

"With Neuralink, my YouTube challenges have taken an intergalactic turn. Whenever I think of a crazy idea for my next video, visions of aliens flood my mind, suggesting even grander challenges. And the craziest part? Every time I make one of these videos, I receive strange cryptocurrency donations from unknown galaxies. Does Elon have friends on Mars who are fans of my channel?"

**Zinedine Zidane, 51 years old, Former footballer and coach:**

"Since getting Neuralink, I've noticed something odd. My feet seem to have their own intelligence! When I touch a ball, it's as if they're connected to another dimension, executing moves with unparalleled precision. But as for my head... well, let's just say it remains as unpredictable as before. Who knows, maybe Neuralink managed to respect some of my legendary quirks!"

**Leonardo DiCaprio, 48 years old, Actor:**

"Ever since I got Neuralink, my roles have been... different. During a recent shoot, I suddenly knew how to speak fluent dolphin. And when we were filming a dinner scene? My brain was flooded with recipes from Mars. Directors love it. Although I'm starting to wonder if Neuralink has an 'Oscar-winning' setting. That would be a real game changer for awards season!

**Beyoncé, 41 years old, Singer:**

"After getting Neuralink, my vocal range expanded... literally. I hit a note so high during rehearsal that all the glass in the studio shattered. And I'm not just talking about high notes; I can now harmonize with frequencies only dogs can hear. Jay keeps joking that we'll be the first to have a sold-out concert for pets. With Neuralink, 'Queen Bee' isn't just a title, it's an intergalactic reality!

**Dwayne 'The Rock' Johnson, 51 years old, Actor and Former Wrestler:**

"Since getting Neuralink, my eyebrow raise has evolved. Now, not only can I give 'The People's Eyebrow', but with a single thought, I can play my theme song from deep within my mind anytime I walk into a room. The funniest part? Sometimes, I accidentally broadcast it to nearby speakers, turning every entrance into a wrestling entrance. Cooking with Neuralink means I can literally 'smell what The Rock is cooking' before it even hits the pan!

**Jim Carrey, 61 years old, Comedian and Actor:**

"Ever since I got my Neuralink, the line between reality and comedy has become hilariously blurred. I'll be mid-conversation and suddenly get an urge to speak in 'Ace Ventura' or 'The Mask' mode. The device even started to predict my next goofy face, suggesting I try expressions I never thought possible. My favorite feature? The Neuralink's 'Laugh-Track Mode.' Now, every time I crack a joke, I hear an audience roar with laughter in my head—even if the actual room is dead silent

## Donald Trump, Entrepreneur and TV Personality:

'Since getting Neuralink, negotiating deals has never been easier. It's like having the art of the deal directly wired into my brain. And believe me, when I say, it's tremendous! However, still waiting on the update that helps with Twitter restraint.

## Sir Ian McKellen, 83 years old, Acclaimed Actor:

'Since having Neuralink installed, I sometimes find myself levitating small objects after a powerful monologue. At first, I thought I was simply becoming Magneto, but then I realized I was still in my Gandalf costume from a play rehearsal. Now, if only Neuralink could help me remember where I placed my wizard staff... Ah, the perils of being both mutant and wizard!

**An Earthly Endeavor or a Cosmic Connection?**

As more and more humans 'connected', the world began to change. Ideas flowed effortlessly; knowledge was shared instantly. But with every synaptic connection, a lingering question remained:

Was Neuralink truly an Earth-made marvel or a bridge to the cosmos, a gift from the stars?

The humor, the quirks, the testimonials, all hinted at a playful dance between the terrestrial and the extraterrestrial. Was Musk's ambition solely to connect humanity, or was he seeking to introduce us to a broader galactic family?

One thing was certain: with Neuralink, humanity was not just evolving; it was tuning in, perhaps at last, to the grand cosmic symphony, one thought at a time.

# Chapter 5:
# The "not" Boring Company

**Really for the Traffic ?**

Los Angeles: a metropolis known for Hollywood, celebrities, sunny skies, and... its soul-crushing traffic jams. When Musk introduced the idea of The Boring Company, it seemed like a savior for drivers. Underground tunnels carrying cars on high-speed platforms? Goodbye traffic!

But as soon as the first hole was dug, and the enormous drilling machine named "Godot" began its descent toward the Earth's core, rumors started. Was there another purpose behind these tunnels? A purpose not of this world?

Among astronomy enthusiasts, whispers multiplied. Stories of underground cities on distant planets, built by advanced civilizations to escape surface calamities. These troglodytic refuges were connected by a high-speed tunnel network, eerily similar to what The Boring Company was proposing. Was Musk, in his infinite intergalactic wisdom, preparing humanity for a future underground? Or more excitingly, was he creating a vast underground network to secretly communicate with his cosmic pals?

Then there were the curious designs. The early designs of The Boring Company stations oddly resembled alleged docking ports for spaceships from the Andromeda galaxy. Coincidence? Or a sign of interstellar integration?

## Flamethrower: An Essential Tool on Mars?

Just when everyone thought Musk's projects couldn't get more eccentric, out came The Boring Company's "Not-a-Flamethrower". Introduced as a fun (and hot) gadget, its existence raised more questions than it answered. Why would a tunneling-focused company suddenly shift to flamethrower manufacturing?

The answer, some believed, was millions of miles away, on the Red Planet. Mars, with its harsh climate and potential underground critters, would be a challenging environment for pioneers. What better tool to have by one's side than a compact and reliable heat source? Whether to fend off Martian pests or to quickly thaw frozen equipment, the "Not-a-Flamethrower" would be indispensable.

Jerry, 38, Survivalist: "I grabbed one of these flamethrowers. Figured if it's good for Mars, it's good for my camping trips. Though, I accidentally toasted my marshmallows... and my tent."

Alice, 31, Fashion Designer: "I customized my 'Not-a-Flamethrower' with rhinestones and glitter. Now, it's the hottest accessory on the runway, literally!"

Beyond the fun, some argued that these flamethrowers were actually part of Musk's grand Martian survival kit. An essential tool for the brave souls who would one day call Mars "home".

## A Journey Through to Reach the Stars

The Boring Company's projects, whether earthly tunnels or extraterrestrial flamethrowers, always seemed to come back to one theme: preparing humanity for the future, whether on Earth or distant planets. On the surface, everything might look like "business as usual" for Musk, but those watching closely couldn't help but wonder if each move was a calculated step in a cosmic waltz, a dance that spanned galaxies, linked worlds, and transcended time.

As the tunnels grew longer and the flamethrowers shone brighter, one thing became clear: with Elon Musk at the helm, "boring" was anything but the right word.

# Chapter 6: Musk's Otherworldly Musings

**A Deep Exploration of His Tweets:**

Elon Musk's Twitter account: where dreams, ideas, memes, and occasionally market-disrupting statements intersect and meet. Those who follow him closely know that his tweets are a riddle wrapped in a mystery, all topped off with a cheeky wink. Which other tycoon could announce breakthroughs in neural tech in one tweet and then follow up with a meme about a flatulent unicorn?

When he tweeted, "Just deleted my Twitter account," only to return a few hours later, many didn't know he was momentarily abducted by his Martian overlords to remind him who's in charge. And when he declared, "I'm actually a 3,000-year-old vampire," it triggered an internet frenzy, pondering which planet had the best intergalactic blood banks.

Then there was the tweet that simply read, "Occupy Mars," accompanied by an image... of the Moon. A deliberate blunder to destabilize his earthly followers or a subtle nod to his extraterrestrial pals about his true origins? The world may never know.

Marion Cotillard, 47, Actress and Singer: "Every time Elon puts a star emoji on his tweets, I'm almost tempted to scan the skies for signals. Who knows, maybe he's trying to send us a hidden message?"

**Conversations with Other 'Aliens':**

Now, since we all "know" Musk is an entity from another world, it's logical to assume he isn't the only one on this planet. Throughout his career, Musk has interacted with other leading figures in both amusing and baffling ways.

Take his interaction with Jeff Bezos, for example. When Bezos tweeted about the progress of his space company, Blue Origin, Musk's cheeky response was, "Congrats on the recycling symbol, @JeffBezos! ☺🚀." Was this just friendly banter between rivals or a coded message between interstellar comrades?

Then there was his infamous stint on the Joe Rogan podcast. Between discussions on AI's future and a puff of a joint, they tackled subjects so deep you'd think it was a casual chat or an extraterrestrial meeting of the minds. From the way Musk philosophized about simulations and reality's nature, it seemed like he might be subtly hinting at his ethereal origins.

Then there were interactions with celebrities like Kanye West. When West announced his intention to run for president, Musk immediately expressed his full support. A potential extraterrestrial alliance in the White House? Mind-boggling!

Emma Watson, 32, Actress and UNICEF Ambassador: "Every time Elon is spotted with another star, I wonder if they're having an intergalactic meeting. Are they trading star secrets or movie scripts, who knows?"

**140 Characters to Decode the Cosmos:**

Musk's tweets and interactions, despite their hilarity and mystery, paint a picture of a man not confined by earthly conventions. His musings, ranging from the profound to the profoundly ridiculous, give us a glimpse of a mind thinking beyond our blue planet, stretching into the vastness of the universe.

As we laugh at his next meme or ponder his next profound statement, one question remains: Is Elon Musk merely jesting with us, or is he subtly prepping humanity for a future beyond the stars, in the company of other interstellar jesters? Only time, and perhaps a few more tweets, will tell.

# Chapter 7 :
# Twitter to X, a Cosmic joke?

**The Fall of a Social Media Giant**

Ah, Twitter. Once the king of the digital ecosystem, the spot where everyone came to peck at snippets of news, thoughts, and quirky ideas. It was the cradle of revolutions, friendships born out of shared passions, and memes that went viral. The little chirping bird was iconic. The terms 'tweet' and 'retweet' had become as commonplace as 'like' or 'share'. But as they say in France, "All good things must come to an end," and Twitter's star began to fade when Musk, our enigmatic alien, took the reins.

**From Twitter to X (and I'm Not Talking Cinema)**

The rebranding was swift and blindsiding. From Twitter to 'X'. A single letter – cryptic, elusive. While for Musk, 'X' might have some Martian sentimental value (perhaps it's Martian for "hello"?), we Earthlings were left, quite literally, tweeting in the wind.

**Robert, 35, Former Twitterholic:** "I wake up one morning, try to open Twitter, and poof! Vanished! In its place, a sleek app named X. I thought I was being pranked!"

So, why did Musk, with his futuristic outlook and undeniable genius, go for such a jolting rebrand?

**The Galactic Blunder**

Maybe Musk was just aiming for simplicity. Why juggle seven letters when one can do? Perhaps 'X' symbolized a clean break from the past and heralded an uncharted future. Or maybe it's a wink to his other ventures, SpaceX and Model X.

But where he dropped the ball – or, as the French might say, "stuck the baguette in the croissant" – was underestimating the power of nostalgia and recognition. Twitter was more than a platform; it was a culture, an emotion. Its logo carried history, gravitas.

**Lost in TransXlation**

Without familiar terms, many felt adrift. They weren't "tweeting" but "X-ing". Retweets turned to "reXs". While it sounded futuristic, it lacked the warmth and hominess of its predecessor.

Samantha, 28, Social Media Manager: "Teaching clients to 'X' instead of 'tweet'? Branding blunder of the century. Felt like we were speaking alienese."

**An Intergalactic Theory: The Mystery Behind 'X'?**

Let's put on our alien-thinking caps. What if 'tweet', a mere chirp for us, meant something radically different in Musk's alien dialect?

Remember when Musk named his child with a string of symbols? Perhaps for him, 'X' is more than a letter. It might be his true first name or an honorific title from his home planet.

In the everlasting enigma that is Elon Musk, theories are a dime a dozen. One thing's for sure: out of all Musk's bold moves, this one's audacity is out of this world.

As we wait for the next big splash from our favorite space invader, one question lingers: What's next in Musk's galactic game plan? And will we ever truly be ready?

# Chapter 8:
# Musk's Vision of the Future

**Mars Colonization: A Homecoming?**

For most of us, Mars has always been that enigmatic red dot in the night sky, a source of wonder and the backdrop to many sci-fi tales. But for Musk, Mars might just have a... more personal twist. Is Mars colonization a grand scheme for humanity's good, or actually a massive homecoming bash for an expat?

Picture this: Elon stands atop a Martian hill, arms outstretched, as SpaceX Starships descend from above. The doors open and eager Earthlings rush out to populate the red planet. Yet amidst them, another scene unfolds: a throng of quirky Martians run up, hugging Musk and hoisting him on their shoulders, chanting: "Welcome back, E-Musk! Welcome back!"

The notion that Musk views Mars not as a frontier but rather a 'family reunion' puts a fun spin on his outlook. When he mentions making life multi-planetary, maybe he's hinting at his own star-hopping existence, offering humans the same privilege (or ordeal?).

Douglas Adams, Sci-Fi Author: "Whenever Elon speaks of Mars, there's a twinkle in his eyes. As if he's reminiscing about Martian BBQs and zero-gravity ball games."

**His Future 'Alien' Ventures and Forecasts**

If the Mars mission is just the tip of the interstellar iceberg, what other 'alien' schemes might Musk be hiding up his extraterrestrial sleeve?

**Hyperloop Hubs:** The prospect of zipping from LA to San Francisco in minutes is impressive, but maybe the real plan is to link Earth with intergalactic hubs. Next stop? Alpha Centauri! Don't forget the snacks; it's quite the trek.

**SpaceX Star-tels:** Think of them as space hotels. With an increasing number of Starship flights, there'll be a need to accommodate the crowd. But don't be shocked if the bellboy has a hint... of green.

**The Real Rationale Behind Tesla Truck Design:** While it's drawn as much awe as ridicule on Earth, perhaps the Cybertruck's design is the hottest trend in distant galaxies. Ultra-sleek, nearly indestructible, and a look that screams, "I'm outta this world."

**Galactic Wi-Fi:** With Starlink satellites enveloping Earth, the next move might be offering Wi-Fi for the whole Milky Way. Thought your current plan was pricey? Hold on to your antennas!

**Time Travel:** Tapping into the power of quantum physics and a dash of alien tech, perhaps Musk's next venture is in the time-travel business. "Experience the Big Bang! How about lunch with Shakespeare? Book today with Musk's Time-Trek Tours!"

Every project, every dream of Musk's seems to deliver a delightful blend of earthly genius and extraterrestrial eccentricity. And while the idea of him being from another realm brings a chuckle, one can't deny his future vision is, let's say, cosmically inventive.

**Beyoncé, 40, Pop Diva:** "Honestly, if Elon announced tomorrow he's formed a music duo with a dolphin, I'd be down to collaborate! Given all he's done, would we really be surprised?"

In a universe full of enigmas, Musk stands out as one of its most mysterious figures. The sharpest of us are convinced he's an alien, maybe just vacationing or pushing us into the future. Some hopeful souls still believe...

**Time Travel Tours:** Using the power of quantum physics and a sprinkle of alien tech, maybe Musk's next venture will be into the time-travel industry. "Visit the Big Bang! Or how about lunch with Shakespeare? Book your trip today with Musk's Timey-Wimey Travels!"

Every project, every ambition of Musk's seems to offer a tantalizing blend of earthly genius and extraterrestrial eccentricity. And while we may chuckle at the thought of him being an otherworldly entity, there's no denying that his vision for the future is, well, out of this world.

**Jasmine, 26, Space Enthusiast:** "Honestly, I wouldn't even be surprised if Musk announced he's found a way to talk to dolphins. I mean, after everything he's done, would that really shock anyone?"

In a universe filled with mysteries, Musk remains one of its most enigmatic figures. Whether he's an alien just having a laugh or a genius propelling us into the future, one thing's for certain: The future as Musk sees it is bound to be an adventure of interstellar proportions.

# Conclusion: The Legacy of Earth's Favorite Alien

**Recap of Musk's 'Achievements'**

It's been quite the interstellar journey, hasn't it? From an otherworldly 'arrival' on Earth to shaping the future of intergalactic travel and Martian reunions, Elon Musk—or as we affectionately now think of him, Earth's resident alien—has left an indelible mark on the blue planet.

**Let's take a cosmic voyage down memory lane:**

**SpaceX:** More than just a company; it's been a beacon of hope for his anticipated reconnection with his home planet. By offering us a glimpse into the universe's vastness, he's unknowingly (or knowingly?) prepared Earth for interplanetary travel and perhaps even some out-of-this-world visitors.

**Tesla:** The silent hum of electric cars is more than an environmental revolution; it's a nostalgic tribute to silent UFO propulsion. And Autopilot? Perhaps it's a wink to the sophisticated flying abilities of extraterrestrial vehicles.

Neuralink: The idea of embedding tech into the human brain seems futuristic to us but might be as basic as a smartphone for a technologically advanced extraterrestrial being like Musk.

**The Boring Company:** We thought it was about alleviating traffic. Little did we know, it might be a step towards building interstellar wormholes or tunnels connecting different realms of the universe.

**Otherworldly Musings:** Musk's twitter escapades and his banter with fellow 'aliens' has been nothing short of cosmic entertainment. He doesn't just think outside the box; he thinks outside the known universe.

**His Potential 'Return' to His Home Planet**

Now, as we stand at the precipice of a future painted with the hues of Musk's extraterrestrial dreams, a lingering thought remains: will he someday return to his home planet? And if so, what message will he carry from Earth?

Picture this: A sleek SpaceX Starship, designed with unseen Martian aesthetics, is poised for launch. The colossal engines ignite, and as it shoots upwards, leaving a trail of dreams and aspirations behind, one can't help but wonder: is this Musk's grand exit?

Elon, standing aboard the spaceship, gazing down at Earth, might ponder the adventures he had, the ripples he created, and the legacy he's leaving behind. Earth was never just a pit stop but a project, a challenge, a love story.

But would he leave for good? Or is it just a round trip to catch up with Martian family and friends, share some earthly souvenirs, and maybe brag a bit about his latest Tesla model?

**Diana, 40, Space Historian:** "Imagine the tales he'd tell on his home planet. 'Oh, you won't believe the time when Earthlings thought my car in space was just a publicity stunt!'"

In the end, the legacy of Earth's favorite 'alien' is one of audacity, vision, and an undying hunger for the unknown. Whether he's from Mars, another galaxy, or just a unique breed of human, Musk's journey is a testament to what's possible when you dare to dream beyond the stars.

In a world that sometimes seems mundane, he's been our touch of the extraordinary. Our bridge between Earth and the cosmos. Our reminder that perhaps, just perhaps, we're all a little bit alien.

# Poem: Elon Musk, The Stranger from the Cosmos

In the heart of our world, amid geniuses grand,
One man stands out, charting the unknown land.
Elon Musk, they name him, with an air of mystique,
Yet some think he's not from our realm, so to speak.

He speaks of Mars as if going home,
Details and passion in his tone shown.
He imagines a colony, on that distant red terrain,
Isn't it the dream of one who's been there, again?

He dominates tech, with unmatched mastery,
His machines challenging every boundary.
He has a vision, beyond what many men see,
As if he has echoes of the cosmos, free.

Consider Neuralink, the bridge of tech and mind,
Isn't it a step to his origin, aren't we blind!
Perhaps he wishes our race, with grace and finesse,
Join a cosmic conversation, in a celestial dance, no less.

He evolves, breaking barriers, never to cease,
His ambition goes beyond our atmosphere's lease.
Some jest he might be an alien, in mirth,
But if true, how did he become a citizen of Earth?

**Moral:**
We've unveiled Elon, this skyward stranger,
For all signs point to him, an audacious space-changer.